The Snowman Joke Book

GW01398577

Other Fun and Puzzle Books available in
Armada

The Teddy Bear Joke Book
Gyles Brandreth

The Dustbin Joke Book
Peter Eldin

A Can Full of Jokes
Jonathan Clements

The Secret Agent's Handbook
Peter Eldin

The Holiday Joke Book
Bill Howard

Writing Jokes and Riddles
Bill Howard

The Snowman
Joke Book

Illustrated by Jo Wright

Armada

An Imprint of HarperCollins*Publishers*

First published in Armada in 1991

Armada is an imprint of
HarperCollins Children's Books,
part of HarperCollins Publishers Ltd
77/85 Fulham Palace Road, Hammersmith,
London W6 8JB

© Complete Editions 1991

Illustrations © Jo Wright 1991

Set in Plantin

Printed and bound in Great Britain by
HarperCollins Manufacturing, Glasgow

ISBN 0 00 694127 3

Conditions of Sale
This book is sold subject to the condition that it
shall not, by way of trade or otherwise, be lent,
re-sold, hired out or otherwise circulated without the
publisher's prior consent in any form of binding or
cover other than that in which it is published and
without a similar condition including this condition
being imposed on the subsequent purchaser.

Introduction

What's round and fat in winter and disappears in summer?
A snowman, of course!

Brrr! This must be the only joke book in the world that makes you shiver and laugh at the same time! That's because it's all about wintry things – snow and ice, Eskimos and polar bears, cold weather and Christmastime, and, of course, snowmen. These pages are so packed with snowmen jokes they form a deep-freeze full of chuckles. So if you want to crack a joke and crack the ice at the same time – read on!

Why did the snowman cut a hole in his
umbrella?
So he could see when it stopped raining.

What do you get if you cross a snowman
with two fish?
A pair of ice skates.

Did you hear about the snowman who
wanted to water ski?
*He failed because no matter how hard he tried
he couldn't find a sloping lake.*

How does a snowman tell the time?
By eating an apple and counting the pips.

What do you do with a snowman who has
water on the knee?
Give him drainpipe trousers.

FAT SNOWMAN: They say travel is
   broadening.
THIN SNOWMAN: Have you been round
   the world, then?

What do people sing at a snowman's birthday party?
"Freeze a jolly good fellow."

FIRST SNOWMAN: That star over there is Mars.
SECOND SNOWMAN: Which star is Pa's, then?

What do you call a snowman's diary at the end of December?
A Yule log.

Twelve snowmen were sheltering under an umbrella but none of them got wet. Why?
Because it wasn't raining.

How does a snowman catch a squirrel?
He climbs up a tree and acts like a nut.

What happened when the snowman stole a
bottle of perfume?
He was convicted of fragrancy.

What happened to the snowman who fell
into a barrel of beer?
He met a bitter end.

HIC!

What's a cold war?
A snowball fight.

What's Indian snow?
Apache here, Apache there.

What's heavy Indian snow?
Apache everywhere.

Knock, knock.
Who's there?
Snow.
Snow who?
Snow use, I can't get in.

What's furry and minty?
A polo bear.

What's an igloo?
An icicle made for two.

An Eskimo mother was telling her small son
a nursery rhyme. "Little Jack Horner sat in
the corner . . ." she began.

Her little boy interrupted her. "Mum," he
asked, "what's a corner?"

What do you call an Eskimo's house without
a loo?
An ig.

An Eskimo had just finished building a new
house. He showed his wife round it and
asked her what she thought of it.

"Ours is an ice house, ours is," she replied.

What do you call an Eskimo wearing five
balaclava hats?
*Anything you like, because he won't be able
to hear you.*

How does Jack Frost get to work?
By icicle.

What's the difference between pack ice and
a clothes brush?
One crushes boats, the other brushes coats.

What happened when the snowman
swallowed a stick of dynamite?
He blew his cool.

Three bears sat on the ice – Mummy,
Daddy and Baby Bear.
  Mummy Bear said, "I have a tale to tell."
  Daddy Bear said, "I have a tale to tell."
  Baby Bear said, "My tail's told."

What's white, wet and travels upwards?
A silly snowflake.

A very fat snowman called Skinner
Said, "How I do wish I were thinner!"
So he sat in the sun
And melted – what fun!
Now he needs a good icy dinner!

What's white and climbs trees?
A snowman (I lied about it climbing trees).

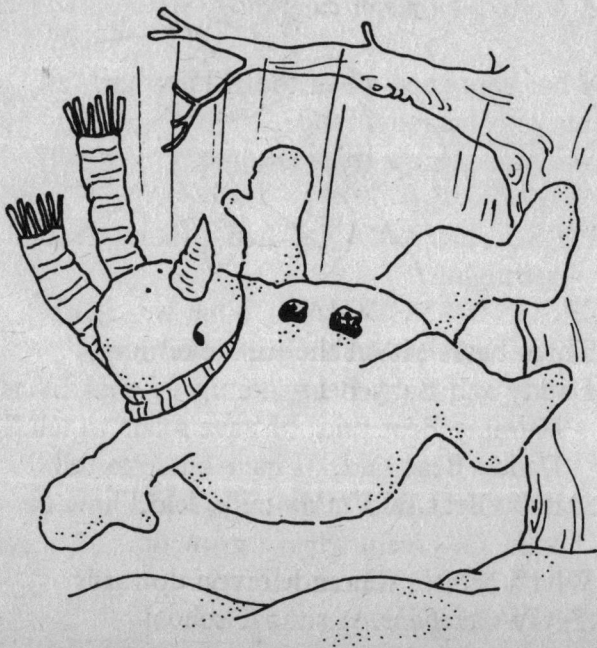

What happens if a snowman has a turned-up nose?
When he sneezes he blows his hat off.

Why don't snowmen eat meat?
No one ever thinks to give them any.

What's a fjord?
A Norwegian motor car.

What happened when the Eskimo girl fell out with her boyfriend?
She gave him the cold shoulder.

FIRST SNOWMAN: I had a funny dream last night.
SECOND SNOWMAN: What was that?
FIRST SNOWMAN: I dreamed I was awake, but when I woke up I found I was asleep.

SNOWCHILD: I'm going to learn how to make ice-cream when I grow up.
SNOWMAN: Where will you do that?
SNOWCHILD: At sundae school.

MARY: Why did the snowman cross the road?

GARY: I don't know. Why did the snowman cross the road?

MARY: To get a Chinese newspaper. Do you get it?

GARY: No.

MARY: Neither do I. I always buy *The Times* myself.

In the middle of a long and very cold winter it snowed for two weeks without stopping, and an isolated cottage on a hillside was completely cut off. Eventually a rescue party managed to dig through the snow and knock at the cottage door.

"Who is it?" called a voice.

"It's the Red Cross," came the reply.

"But I've already given you money this winter!" came the response.

What happened to the snowmen who met in a revolving door?

They went around together for quite a long time.

Where does a three-tonne polar bear sleep?
Anywhere it wants to.

How does an Eskimo build a house?
I-gloos it together.

HIL: I'll just go out and check the snowman.
PHIL: I'd rather have him white.

What did Chief Running Water call his baby?
Little Drip.

What did Chief Running Water call his baby in winter?
Little Icicle.

FRED: My father was a Pole.
TED: North or South?

What do polar bears have for supper?
Icebergers.

This must be what people call a liquid diet!

FIRST SNOWMAN: You used to live in
  Scotland, didn't you?
SECOND SNOWMAN: That's right.
FIRST SNOWMAN: The scenery must
  have been lovely.
SECOND SNOWMAN: I don't know. I
  couldn't see most of it for the mountains.

What did the snowman say when William
Tell fired at him?
"That was an arrow escape!"

An incompetent snowman called Scott
Tried crossing the Channel by yacht.
Gales blew him off course
So he tapped out in Morse
"Dot, dot, dot, dash, dash, dash, dot, dot, dot."

How does a snowman prevent his hands
from melting when he washes them?
He wears rubber gloves.

What fur does a snowman get from a skunk?
As fur as possible.

Do snowmen go on safari?
Not safaris I know.

When a traveller got lost in the mountains of
Switzerland, a St Bernard dog with a brandy
keg round its neck was sent out to rescue
him. Eventually it returned, with an empty
brandy flask and a note saying, "Brandy
excellent, please send cigar."

FARMER'S WIFE: What's the weather
  like?
FARMER: Below freezing.
FARMER'S WIFE: How can you tell?
FARMER: When I milked the cows I got
  ice-cream.

What do Eskimo farmers do in winter?
Snow-plough their fields.

ESKIMO BOY: Where does your mum
   come from?
ESKIMO GIRL: Alaska.
ESKIMO BOY: Don't worry, I'll ask her
   myself.

Why did the mean man buy six bottles of
antifreeze?
To avoid having to buy a winter coat.

What kind of fish is useful in winter?
A skate.

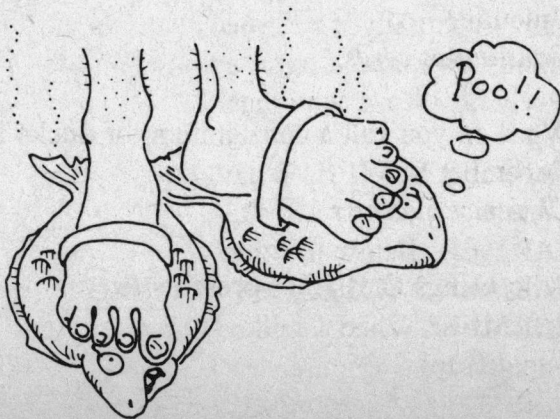

Poo!!

Mary Christmas is, of course, Father Christmas's wife. Christmas is a very good time for jokes, because it's a time when we see our friends and go to parties, and there are lots of very funny jokes about Christmas. Here are some of them.

FIRST SNOWMAN: My throat's sore. I think I've got tinselitis.
SECOND SNOWMAN: You mean tonsilitis.
FIRST SNOWMAN: No, tinselitis. I ate some of the Christmas decorations.

What do angry rodents send each other at Yuletide?
Cross-mouse cards.

What do you call a consignment of ducks in December?
Christmas quackers.

Who brings Christmas presents to detectives?
Santa Clues.

DAVE: I forgot to send my sister a card at Christmas.
MAVE: What did she say?
DAVE: Nothing yet.

What do you call a reindeer wearing a number plate?
Reg.

What are the best things to put in a
Christmas pudding?
Your teeth.

Mr & Mrs Eggberger were over from
America on a winter holiday in Moscow.
They were being shown round the Kremlin
by their guide, Rudolf.

Mr Eggberger looked out of the window.
"It's snowing," he remarked.

Rudolf looked out of the window too.
"No," he said. "That's not snow, that's rain."

"I'm sure it's snow," persisted Mr
Eggberger.

His wife interrupted. "I'm sure Rudolf the
Red knows rain, dear," she said.

What do you call it when people hold a tug
of war on 31 December?
A New Year's 'eave.

What has the shortest lifespan in the world?
*A New Year's resolution. It is born before
midnight and dead and forgotten the
following day.*

GERT: And where did you spend
  Christmas?
BERT: In jail.
GERT: In jail? Whatever for?
BERT: I got caught when I was doing some
  early Christmas shopping.
GERT: What's wrong with that? When were
  you doing it?
BERT: At two o'clock in the morning.

What do you get if you cross a turkey with
an octopus?
I don't know, but everyone gets a leg at
Christmas!

How many chimneys does Santa go down?
Stacks.

What do monkeys sing at Christmas?
"Jungle Bells".

MRS JONES: We're having Uncle Herbert
  for Christmas dinner.
MRS BONES: Really? We always have a
  turkey.

Why does Santa Claus climb down chimneys?
Because it soots him.

LIZZIE: I was going to buy you some hankies for Christmas.
LIZZIE'S AUNT: Why didn't you, dear?
LIZZIE: Because I couldn't remember how big your nose was.

Cuthbert was born on 24 December.
He wanted to be home for Christmas.

BOB: I'll tell you what I like about Christmas - kissing the girls under the mistletoe.
ROB: Do you? I prefer kissing them under the nose.

What do the British call Christmas?
Yule Britannia.

What exams did Santa take before he could do his job?
Ho-ho-ho levels.

Overheard one Christmas Eve: "I don't care who you are, you fat, bearded old man, just get these dratted deer off my roof!"

What's the cheapest way to get to Lapland?
Be born there.

FIRST SNOWMAN: How old are you?
SECOND SNOWMAN: Sixty-two.
FIRST SNOWMAN: That's an ice age, isn't it?

Where do flies go in winter?
To the glassworks, to be turned into bluebottles.

How do people dress at the North Pole?
Quickly!

SAMMY: Boo hoo! Boo hoo!
TEACHER: What's the matter, Sammy?
SAMMY: I can't find my boots in the cloakroom.
TEACHER: Are you sure these aren't yours?
SAMMY: Quite sure. You see, mine had snow on them.

Who was Snow White's brother?
Egg White. Get the yolk?

What is Florence Penguin's nickname?
Ice-floe.

What's boiled, cooled, sweetened then soured?
Iced tea with lemon.

What did one Christmas cracker say to another?
"My pop's bigger than your pop."

When a girl slips on the ice, why can't her brother help her up?
Because he can't be her brother and assist her (a sister) too.

What happened when someone put sunglasses on the snowman?
He took a dim view of everything.

Life has gotten so dull lately!

What never gets any wetter no matter how
much it rains?
The sea.

Why did the little boy stick sugar lumps in
the snowman?
So he would have sweet dreams.

What do you call a Scottish snowman who
lives in Switzerland?
MacAlpine.

LUCY: Did you hear about the snowmen
    who were painters? One had a tin of red
    paint and one had a tin of brown paint, and
    they bumped into each other and the paint
    got spilled.
LENNY: What happened then?
LUCY: They were marooned.

There was once a snowlady called Emma
Who was seized with a terrible tremor.
She had swallowed a spider
Which wriggled inside her –
Oh dear, what an awful dilemma!

How does a snowman get into a locked
garden shed?
He sings until he finds the right key.

Three men got stuck in a snowdrift, but
only one got his hair wet. Why?
The other two were bald.

ANNIE: You've put Ben's Easter tie on the
  snowman.
DANNY: Why do you call it his Easter tie?
ANNIE: Because it's got egg all over it.

What's ice?
Skid stuff.

ESKIMO BOY TO ESKIMO GIRL:
What's an ice girl like you doing in a place
like this?

Knock, knock.
Who's there?
Ski.
Ski who?
Ski's a jolly good fellow.

Two Eskimos were discussing the previous winter. One said, "It was so cold our candles froze and we couldn't blow them out."

The other replied, "That's nothing. Where we lived it was so cold our words came out frozen and we had to thaw them over the fire to find out what we were saying."

Two snowmen were watching the sea. One asked, "Why doesn't the sea fall over the horizon?"

The second replied, "It's tide."

What sheet cannot be folded?
A sheet of ice.

Why do Eskimos eat whale meat and
blubber?
You'd blubber if you had to eat whale meat!

GEOGRAPHY TEACHER: Lapland is very
   thinly populated.
TOMMY: How many Lapps are there to the
   mile, Miss?

There's a man at the door
collecting for our new village swimming
pool. Shall I give him our snowman?

Why are pine trees always warm?
Because they're fir trees.

FIRST SNOWMAN: I bet I know where
  I'm going tonight.
SECOND SNOWMAN: Where?
FIRST SNOWMAN: To sleep.

What do you call a black Eskimo dog?
A dusky husky.

A child came along with two carrots to
make noses for the snowmen. One was
a bright orange juicy carrot, the other
an old, wizened one. But just as she was
going to put them on their faces she was
called in to lunch. So the snowmen decided
to share them out. The larger snowman
picked up the wizened carrot and gave it to
his companion. "Humph!" said the second
snowman. "If I'd been handing out the
carrots I'd have given you the better one!"

"Well, that's what I've done," said
the first snowman, "so what are you
complaining about?"

Good King Wenceslas looked out,
On the feast of Stephen.
A snowball hit him on the snout,
Made it all uneven.
Brightly shone his conk that night,
And the pain was cruel,
Till a doctor came in sight,
Riding on a mu-u-el.

What stays hot in a snowman's house?
Mustard.

MAISIE: What animal can jump higher than a snowman?
DAISY: Er, a kangaroo?
MAISIE: Any animal – a snowman can't jump.

Why do unemployed actors long to slip on the ice?
Because if they broke a leg they'd be in a cast for weeks.

FIRST SNOWCHILD: Why did you give up your tap dancing lessons?
SECOND SNOWCHILD: I kept falling in the sink.

When is it stupid to learn a language?
When you begin Finnish.

Knock, knock.
Who's there?
Wendy.
Wendy who?
Wendy red, red, robin comes bob-bob-bobbing along.

Did you hear that the Greeks invented the deep freeze, but didn't think the idea worth Parthenon?

What can travel through a snowstorm without getting wet?
A ray of sunlight.

FIRST SNOWMAN: Do you always snore?
SECOND SNOWMAN: Only when I'm asleep.

Why wasn't the snowman hurt when a barrel of beer fell on him?
It was light ale.

Two snowmen were talking together in the garden. "This family's very rich, you know," said the first.
"How do you know?" asked the second.
"They have three swimming pools."
"Why three?"
"One hot, one cold and one empty."
"What's the empty one for?"
"For people who can't swim."

What did the deaf fisherman get for
Christmas?
A herring aid.

What did the hippie snowman say when his
cat came in from the cold?
"Cool cat!"

TED: Is it snowing outside?
TINA: I don't know. Send Rover out and
 see if he comes in with snowflakes on his
 coat.

What happens when you slip and fall down
on the ice?
Your bottom gets thaw.

Throb-Throb

41

Who discovered fire?
Oh, some bright spark.

Who invented the fireplace?
Alfred the Grate.

Why is a snowman like a cowboy?
Because an Indian would call him a paleface.

What does a snowman overlook?
His nose.

What's higher than a snowman?
His hat.

Why do Eskimos eat candles?
For light refreshment.

FIRST SNOWMAN: Have you heard the
   weather forecast for tomorrow?
SECOND SNOWMAN: Yes. They say it
   will be dry and sunny and . . .
FIRST SNOWMAN: Oh dear.
SECOND SNOWMAN: . . . there's a 90
   per cent chance they're wrong.

How do you make antifreeze?
Hide her jumpers.

When does it rain money?
When there's a change in the weather.

What are Eskimos parents male and female children called?
Blubber and sister.

SNOWLADY: Do you think I'm vain?
SNOWMAN: No. Why do you ask?
SNOWLADY: Because snowladies as good-looking as me usually are.

What kind of money do Eskimos use?
Ice lolly.

What lives in winter, grows with its roots upwards, and dies in summer?
An icicle.

What falls down in winter but doesn't get hurt?
Snow.

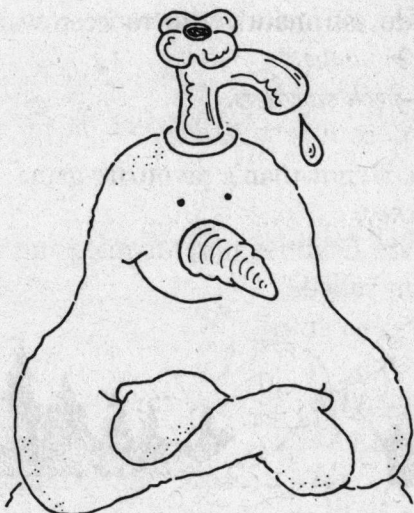

Try saying this three times quickly: Sam the
Snowman snored sleepily and slipped on
stones slippy with snow.

Have you read:
The Solitary Snowman by I. Malone
and
Ice Houses by S. Keemo?

What do astronauts wear to keep warm in winter?
Apollo-neck sweaters.

What's a snowman's favourite game?
Ice hockey.

Why is it difficult to keep a secret on a very cold day?
Because your teeth chatter.

Why did the snow-drop?
Because it heard the cro-cus.

FIRST SNOWMAN: There's one good
  thing about smog.
SECOND SNOWMAN: What's that?
FIRST SNOWMAN: You can see what
  you're breathing.

When is a boat like a fall of snow?
When it's adrift.

Why should you never put the letter "M" in
the fridge?
Because it turns "ice" into "mice".

What did the snowman say to the rain?
*"If you keep this up much longer my name
will be slush."*

Mr Featherbrain had gone to visit his friend
Mr Peabrain. When it was time for him to
leave they discovered it was snowing hard,
so Mr Peabrain kindly said Mr Featherbrain
could stay the night.

    "That's very kind of you," said Mr
Featherbrain. "I'll just nip home and fetch
my toothbrush."

BABY POLAR BEAR: Am I a real polar bear?

MOTHER POLAR BEAR: Of course, dear.

BABY POLAR BEAR: Are you sure?

MOTHER POLAR BEAR: Yes. Why do you ask?

BABY POLAR BEAR: Because the cold is killing me!

What do you get when two French prams collide in the snow?
A crèche.

What's the use of reindeer?
Makes the flowers grow, darling.

Old snowmen never die, they just lose their cool.

ED: Why is that snowman wearing a red hat like a biscuit?
FRED: Because he's a ginger nut.

How do snowmen slim?
They stand out in the rain.

Which animal is it best to be in a snowstorm with?
A little otter.

FIRST SNOWMAN: What's five Q and five Q?
SECOND SNOWMAN: Ten Q.
FIRST SNOWMAN: You're welcome.

Mrs Brown was dressing her small son Timmy so he could go and play out in the snow, but Timmy was very anxious to be off and kept fidgeting. So she told him a story about a little boy who wanted to go out and play with his sledge in the snow but refused to put on his outdoor clothes, so he caught a chill and died.

"Oh, Mum", said Timmy, his eyes shining, "what happened to his sledge?"

No one has ever seen a Yeti, or Abominable Snowman, but they have found footprints in the Himalayas they believe are those of a large monster. You can create your own Abominable Snowman footprints on a snowy lawn by walking around holding buckets on your feet, and carrying a walking stick or broom handle, with which, at each step, you draw "claw" marks. The resulting "footprints" look like those of a large bear.

However, if you haven't got any snow, you can still enjoy these Abominable Snowmen jokes.

What do owls sing when its snowing?
"Too wet to woo."

What happens when it rains beer?
You get an ale storm.

What's worse than raining cats and dogs?
Hailing taxis.

Have you read:
Out in the Snow and the Rain by Anna Rack

Holly and Dolly were going out sledging in the snow. Their mother had told them they must share the sledge equally, knowing Holly, who was older, was a bit of a bully.

When they got back, she asked Holly if she had let her sister share the sledge. "Oh yes," replied Holly. "We shared it equally, as you said. I had it going downhill, and Dolly had it going uphill."

Two fat snowmen ran in a race.
One ran in short bursts, the other in burst shorts.

What does a snowman say when he tells
a joke?
"This one'll sleigh you."

What do Abominable Snowmen call their
babies?
Chill-dren.

What did the Abominable Snowman eat
after his teeth were pulled out?
The dentist.

Why did the Abominable Snowman send his
father to Siberia?
Because he wanted frozen pop.

Why were the Abominable Snowman's
fingers never more than eleven inches long?
*Because if they were twelve inches long
they'd be feet.*

What happened when the boy Abominable
Snowman met the girl Abominable
Snowman?
They fell in love at first fright.

What's an Abominable Snowman's last drink?
His bier.

What jewels do Abominable Snowmen wear?
Tombstones.

Why did the bald Abominable Snowman stick his head out of the window?
To get some fresh 'air.

Did you hear about the girl Abominable Snowman who wasn't pretty and wasn't ugly?
She was pretty ugly.

Why did the Abominable Snowman buy two tickets at the zoo?
One to get in and one to get out.

What does an Abominable Snowman do when he loses a hand?
Goes to a secondhand store.

Where do Abominable Snowmen dance?
At snowballs.

Why did the Abominable Snowman give up boxing?
Because he didn't want to spoil his looks.

54

Why did the Abominable Snowman go to a psychiatrist?
Because he thought everyone was beginning to like him.

How do you make an Abominable Snowman shrink?
Feed him on condensed milk.

What did one Abominable Snowman say to the other?
"I'm afraid I just don't believe in people."

HA! HA! HA!

What's white and melts in front of the fire?
Ice-cream.

GRANNY PERKINS: Last winter I wore a
  white coat so I could be seen by the traffic
  on gloomy days.
GRANNY PETERKINS: What a good idea.
GRANNY PERKINS: It wasn't really. You
  see, I got knocked down by a snowplough.

MARY: If frozen water is iced water, what
  is frozen ink?
MANDY: Iced ink.
MARY: I know you do!

What goes in pink and comes out blue?
A mid-winter swimmer.

What's an Abominable Snowman's favourite
book?
War and Frozen Peas.

How do you greet an Abominable Snowman
with three heads?
"Hello, hello, hello!"

What kind of Abominable Snowman has the
best hearing?
The eeriest.

How do monster snowmen feel when they
melt?
Abominable!

FIRST ESKIMO: That cough of yours is
  making you bark your head off.
SECOND ESKIMO: Yes, I admit I'm a
  little husky.

Mary had a little lamb
It was a greedy glutton.
She fed it on ice-cream all day
and now it's frozen mutton.

Why do you feel cold if you lose your two
front teeth?
You have no central eating.

Which airline do Abominable Snowmen fly
on?
British Scareways.

What do you get if you cross a lion with a
snowman?
Frostbite.

How do you confuse a naughty Eskimo
child?
Tell him to stand in the corner of his igloo.

What's a snowman given on his birthday?
An iced cake.

Knock, knock.
Who's there?
Snow.
Snow who?
Snow shoes are useful in this weather.

What has two humps and is found at the
North Pole?
A camel with no sense of direction.

Mrs Huntingdon-Smythe had just got a new au pair girl from Lapland. On her first day of work she asked her to go and make the children's beds and dust the bedrooms.

"Please, I do not know how to make beds or dust," said the au pair.

"Well, in that case, go into the kitchen and start getting the food ready for lunch," said Mrs Huntingdon-Smythe.

"Please, I do not know how to cook," said the au pair.

"Well, if you can't make beds or dust, and you can't cook, what can you do?" asked the harassed housewife.

The au pair smiled. "I can milk a reindeer," she said proudly.

FIRST SNOWMAN: Who's that lady with the little wart?
SECOND SNOWMAN: Shh, that's her husband.

What does a snowman do when he wears out his trousers?
Wears them in again.

60

What does a schoolboy snowman wear on his head?
An icecap.

After their ship had sunk, two shivering shipwrecked sailors climbed on to an ice floe and hoped that help would arrive. They had been there some time and were almost dying of cold, when one of them began to despair. "Do you think help will ever arrive?" he asked.

His companion pointed to the horizon. "It's coming now," he said, as a ship hove into view. "It's a ship called the *Titanic*."

What would a snowman get if he fell in the Thames?
Wet.

What happens to a snowman who walks fifty miles?
He gets foot thaw.

TRACEY: A snowman wanted to cross a river. There was no bridge, no boat, and if he tried to wade across he'd melt. How did he get across?
STACEY: I give up.
TRACEY: So did the snowman.

What happened to the man who dreamed he was eating the biggest ice-cream in the world?
He woke up to find himself eating a snowman.

Two snowmen in a garden were wondering what happened to the sun when it set. They wondered and pondered all night – and then it finally dawned on them.

A man driving to work on an icy morning
skidded and his car hit a wall. He got out
to look at the damage, and his friend, who
was passing, stopped to see if he could help.

"Oh dear, it does look bad," said the friend,
looking at the crumpled front wing and
ripped-off bumper.

The driver shook his head philosophically.
"That's just the way the Mercedes Benz, I'm
afraid," he said.

How does a snowman greet a friend?
"Hail!"

What did the North Wind say to the South
Wind?
"Let's play draughts."

What is wind?
Air in a hurry.

If there are fifty-two weeks in a year, how
many seconds are there?
Twelve – January 2nd, February 2nd, etc.

What do you call an Arctic cow?
An Eskimoo.

MOO!!

Why is a pet polar bear cheap to feed?
Because it lives on ice.

Who's a snowman's favourite TV
personality?
David Frost.

Where do snowmen like to live?
Iceland.

TED: Is that a snowman or a snow-woman?
FRED: I can't tell if it's a he or a ski.

What do snowmen fish for?
Frozen fish fingers.

Which month has twenty-eight days?
They all do.

Which travels faster, heat or cold?
Heat. You can catch cold.

What bow can't be tied?
A rainbow.

TEACHER: What came after the Ice Age?
SILLY SUE: Er, the saus-age, Miss?

TEACHER: Give me the name of a liquid
   that won't freeze.
JENNY: Hot water, Miss.

Knock, knock.
Who's there?
Felix.
Felix who?
Felix my ice-cream again I'll punch him!

What happened to the snowman who
swallowed uranium?
He got atomic-ache.

66

HENRY: Look at the snowman! He's on the telly!
HERBERT: How did he get there?
HENRY: I think he climbed up from the sofa.

FIRST SNOWMAN: I could marry anyone I please.
SECOND SNOWMAN: Then why don't you?
FIRST SNOWMAN: I haven't pleased anyone yet.

Why did the snowman stand on his head?
He was turning things over in his mind.

Some lucky people go off on winter sports holidays in winter. Join them on a hilarious tour of the ski slopes, the airports, the railway stations, the hotels, and all the other places that are part of a holiday abroad.

JENNY: I flew to Switzerland last year.
KENNY: Didn't your arms get tired?

NERVOUS PASSENGER ON AIRCRAFT:
  You will get me down safely, won't you?
PILOT: I've never left anyone up there yet.

Why did the snowman paint himself gold?
He had a gilt complex.

BUS PASSENGER: Do you stop at the
  Hilton Hotel?
BUS CONDUCTOR: On my salary? Are
  you kidding?

What's Norway like?
Sweden without the matches.

A school party was about to board a ship to sail to Norway for their skiing holiday. Before they embarked, their head teacher gave them a lecture on safety. "Now, children," she said, "what would you do if one of you fell overboard?"

"Shout 'child overboard', Miss," they replied.

"Good. And what would you do if a teacher fell overboard?" she asked.

There was a thoughtful silence. "Er, which one?" asked a brave pupil.

PASSENGER: How can I be sure the trains are running on time?

RAILWAY OFFICIAL: Just before one comes into the station, put your watch on the track.

TRAVELLER: Cabby! How much to drive me to the airport?

CAB DRIVER: £20, sir.

TRAVELLER: And how much for my suitcase?

CAB DRIVER: Oh, there's no charge for that, sir.

TRAVELLER: In that case, just take the
  suitcase. I'll walk.

PASSENGER: Does this train stop at
  Zermatt?
RAILWAY OFFICIAL: If it doesn't there'll
  be an almighty crash!

What's the hardest thing about learning to
ski?
The ground.

GLORIA: So you're not going to Davos for
   your winter sports holiday this year?
GORDON: No, that was last year. This year
   we're not going to the Tyrol.

Mr & Mrs Feather had just arrived at
the airport in time to catch their plane to
Austria.
   "Oh dear," said Mrs Feather. "I wish I'd
brought the hall table with us."
   "Whatever for?" asked Mr Feather.
"Because the plane tickets are on it," his wife
replied sadly.

TRAVELLER: Is the train on time?
STATION MASTER: We're happy if it's on
   the track, sir.

HARRY: How long have you been learning
   to skate?
LARRY: Oh, about a dozen sittings.

MRS BRAKE: Our hotel was so overbooked
   we had to sleep on a door across two tables.
MRS ANKEL: How uncomfortable!

Heavily laden with suitcases, a traveller
ran on to the station platform and sprinted
after the train, which was just pulling out of
the station. He stood there, red in the face,
puffing and panting. A sympathetic porter
said, "Just missed the train, did you, sir?"

"No," fumed the man. "I didn't like the
look of it so I chased it out of the station."

How can you tell when a train has gone?
It leaves tracks behind.

When would you be glad to be down and out?
After a bumpy flight in a plane.

The aircraft had just taken off and was flying at 30,000 feet over the Alps. A voice came over the intercom: "This is your captain speaking. Sit back and relax and enjoy your flight. This is a totally automatic plane. It flies on automatic pilot, it serves drinks and meals automatically, it lands automatically. Nothing can go wrong with it, go wrong with it go wrong with it . . . ."

BROTHER: Gosh, look at all the people down there. They look just like ants.
SISTER: They *are* ants, silly. We haven't taken off yet.

JADED SKIER: I don't know why they say après-ski is fun. I ache all over and I'm covered in bruises.

What's the last word in aeroplanes?
"Jump!"

Jason was terrified of flying and decided to travel to Italy for his winter sports holiday by coach. The trouble was, the coach had an accident. A plane landed on it.

What's the difference between a bus driver and a cold?
One knows the stops, the other stops the nose.

What's a volcano?
A mountain that blows its cool.

FIRST SNOWMAN: My girlfriend's one of twins.
SECOND SNOWMAN: How do you tell them apart?
FIRST SNOWMAN: Her brother has a beard.

FIRST SNOWMAN: Do you think it will rain?
SECOND SNOWMAN: That rather depends on the weather, doesn't it?

BETTY: Why are you paddling in your socks?
HETTIE: The water's cold in January.

TRAVELLER: Yes, this is quite nice but I really wanted a room with a bath.
HOTEL CLERK: This isn't your room, sir, *this is the lift*.

HOTEL MANAGER: I hope you enjoyed your stay here. sir.
HOTEL GUEST: Yes, I did, but I'm sorry to have to leave the hotel so soon after practically buying it.

MRS SMITH: Does this plane fly faster than sound?
AIR HOSTESS: No, madam.
MRS SMITH: Oh good. My friend and I want to talk.

PRUE: How did you break your leg?
SUE: You see that ice on the kitchen steps?
PRUE: Yes.
SUE: I didn't.

How does a snowman stop a head cold going to his chest?
Ties a knot in his neck.

What happens when a Fairy Snow-man gets caught in the rain?
He turns into a lot of bubbles.

TEACHER: What is the weather like in New Zealand?
CHRIS: Very cold.
TEACHER: Why do you say that?
CHRIS: 'Cos when they send us meat it's always frozen.

Knock, knock.
Who's there?
Police.
Police who?
Police let me in, it's freezing out here.

FIRST SNOWMAN: How do you keep an idiot in suspense?

SECOND SNOWMAN: I don't know.
FIRST SNOWMAN: I'll tell you next week.

JOHN: Did anyone laugh when you fell on the ice?

RON: No, but the ice made some terrible cracks.

Little Sammy was scribbling on a piece of paper.

"What are you doing?" asked his mother.

"Writing a letter to the snowman," replied Sammy.

"But you can't write yet!" exclaimed his mother.

"That's all right," said Sammy happily. "The snowman can't read."

What's a description of hail?
Hard-boiled rain.

What did the artist snowman paint?
A frieze around the room.

FIRST SNOWMAN: It's gone, gone
  forever!
SECOND SNOWMAN: What has?
FIRST SNOWMAN: Yesterday.

What can run across the floor without any
legs?
Water.

What did the speak-your-weight machine say
when the snowman stepped on it?
"One at a time, please."

What's the inside of a frozen chicken called?
A blizzard.

Did you hear about the snowman who
dreamed he was eating three small, hard
biscuits?
*When he woke up he found his jacket
buttons had disappeared!*

What's a lazy snowman's hobby?
Sitting in a corner collecting snowflakes.

What do you call a snowman with a
calculator in his boots?
Smarty-boots.

"Doctor, doctor, I feel like a snowman!"
"Keep cool."

FIRST SNOWMAN: I can't get this match
  to light.
SECOND SNOWMAN: What's wrong with
  it?
FIRST SNOWMAN: I don't know. It lit
  this morning.

Knock, knock.
Who's there?
Max.
Max who?
Max keep the snow off.

What's the definition of ice-skating?
Skids' play.

How do you make a Swiss roll?
Push him off an Alp.

BOB: Lightning never strikes the same
   snowman twice.
ROB: No, if it strikes him once he won't be
   there any more!

Why do birds fly south in winter?
Because it's too far to walk.

DILLY: Mum, when did Julius Caesar
   reign?
MUM: I didn't know he reigned.
DILLY: Of course he did. Didn't they all
   shout, "Hail, Caesar!"?

Two snowmen were watching the sun set into the snow-covered horizon.

"Doesn't the sun look wonderful?" said one.

"Yes, but there won't half be a fizzle when it hits the snow," replied the other.

What should a snowman take when a car runs into it?
The car's registration number.

What do you get if you cross a football team with ice-cream?
Aston Vanilla.

What did the dog say when he sat down on
the gritted icy road?
"Rough!"

What do you get if you build a snow dog
and it melts?
A slush puppy.

When is a boat like a pile of snow?
When it's adrift.

How does a fire feel when you've loaded it
up with coal?
Grate-ful.

If you look round on a cold winter's day,
what do you see on every hand?
A glove.

What kind of bow can't be tied?
A rainbow.

What goes up when the snow comes down?
An umbrella.

What do you get if you sleep under an
electric blanket that's too hot?
Sideburns.

Knock, knock.
Who's there?
Ammonia.
Ammonia who?
Ammonia poor little snowman.

Two snowmen were standing in the garden
during a terrible thunderstorm. One turned
to the other and said, "Is that man in the
house messing about with the television
again?"

Where do Eskimos keep their huskies?
In mush-rooms.

ADVERTISEMENT IN NEWSPAPER:
For sale, fridge-freezer suitable for young
lady with light inside.

How did Noah light the Ark?
By flood-lights.

How do children know when the school
holidays are over?
It stops raining.

What gloves can you never wear in winter?
Foxgloves.

Why do guardsmen catch cold easily?
*Because they're always out in their
bearskins.*

How did the snowman use a piece of rope to
forecast the weather?
*When it swung it knew it was windy, when
it hung very still it knew it was freezing.*

How do you get cool music?
Put your radio in the fridge.

How do you stop an ice-lolly dropping out
of your mouth?
Grit your teeth.

What game can you play in water?
Swimming pool.

What's the coldest country in the world?
Chile.

Knock, knock.
Who's there?
Martini.
Martini who?
Martini hand is frozen, let me in.

What is ice?
Hard water.

What is heavier in warm weather than in cold?
Traffic to the beach.

Jason had been on a skiing holiday. When he returned his friend Jonathan said he must have had a good time, as he'd got a marvellous tan.

"Tan!" exclaimed Jason. "We never saw the sun – it rained all the time! This isn't a tan, it's rust!"

What does a ship say at the North Pole?
"Shiver me timbers!"

FIRST SNOWMAN: Why are you so
  angry?
SECOND SNOWMAN: It's all the rage.

What is someone whose father was born
in Iceland and whose mother was born in
Cuba?
An ice cube.

What's fat, white and lifts weights?
An extra-strong snowman.

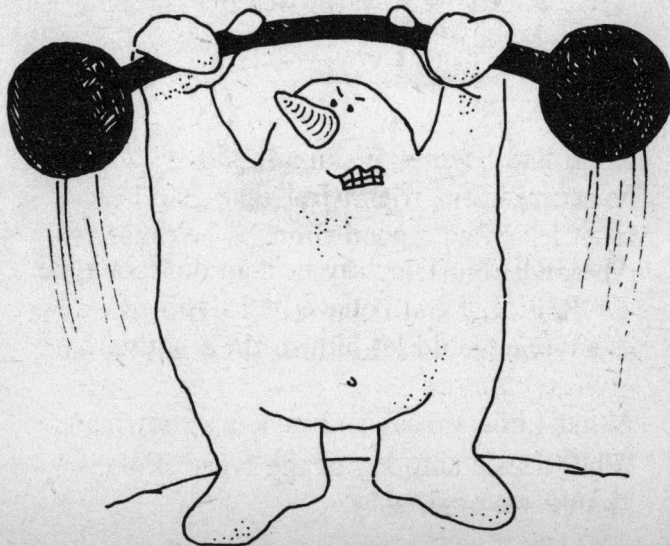

What's the height of impossibility?
A snowman trying to get a suntan.

HERE LIE
THE REMAINS OF
A
VERY
STUPID
SNOWMAN
R.I.P.

MAUREEN: They say he's an outdoor type.
DOREEN: I can believe it. I doubt if
  anyone would let him in their house.

What's hot, greasy and makes a snowman
melt?
A chip on his shoulder.

Have you read:
Winter Weather by Gail N. Snow
Winter Landscape by Theresa Bear
and
Central Heating by Ray D. Ater?

What does a snowman do when he has
stomach trouble?
*Keeps his coat buttoned up and hopes no
one notices.*

TEACHER: Give me an example of heat
   expanding and cold contracting.
SHEILA: Hot summer days are longer than
   cold winter ones.

MIKE: What hat shall we put on the
   snowman?
SPIKE: Dad's pork-pie hat?
MIKE: No, the gravy might melt him.

DEL: I never had a sledge when I was a
   child. We couldn't afford one.
MEL: What did you do in the snow?
DEL: Slid down hills on my brother.

Why is a snowman like a plastic surgeon?
They both melt if they sit by the fire.

The night was growing dark and cold
As she trudged through snow and sleet.
Her nose was long and cold,
And her shoes were full of feet.

What do you get if you cross an elephant
with an Abominable Snowman?
A jumbo yeti.

How do you make a Mexican chilli?
Take him to the South Pole.

What happened when the snake caught a
cold?
She adder viper nose.

BANK MANAGER: You can't open an
  account with a piece of wood!
LUMBERJACK: But I wanted to open a
  shavings account.

What did the lumberjack do on Christmas
Eve?
He went on a chopping spree.

How did the world's tallest snowman
become short overnight?
Somebody stole all his money.

What sort of man doesn't like to sit in front
of the fire?
A snowman.

FIRST SNOWMAN: Did you hear the joke
  about the eggs?
SECOND SNOWMAN: No.
FIRST SNOWMAN: Two bad.

What do you call an Eskimo with a radiator
on top of her head?
Anita.

A snowman was singing, and he didn't have much of a voice. His companion said to him, "Do you know 'Loch Lomond'?"

"Yes," replied the singing snowman.

"Then go and jump in it," retorted his friend.

FIRST SNOWMAN: A noise woke me up this morning.
SECOND SNOWMAN: What noise?
FIRST SNOWMAN: The crack of dawn.

When is a window like a star?
When it's a skylight.

What causes a flood?
A river that's too big for its bridges.

Why do you run faster when you have a cold?
Because you have a racing pulse and a running nose.

What sweets do skiers enjoy?
Glacier mints.

"Doctor, doctor, I feel like an ice-cream!"
"So do I, shall we go out and buy some?"

How does a snowman start work as a
farmer?
He uses a snowplough.

FIRST SNOWMAN: I see more of Harold
  than I used to.
SECOND SNOWMAN: Yes, they've added
  to him recently.

How do sheep keep warm in Siberia?
Central bleating.

Why was the snowman's dog called Frost?
Because Frost bites.

FIRST SNOWMAN: There's only one way
  to make money.
SECOND SNOWMAN: What's that?
FIRST SNOWMAN: I might have known
  you wouldn't know it!

What's the difference between ammonia and
pneumonia?
*One comes in bottles and the other in
chests.*

Knock, knock.
Who's there?
Dawn.
Dawn who?
Dawn leave me standing out here in the cold.

Who gets a warm reception wherever he
    goes?
A fireman.

Where do Eskimos keep their money?
In snow banks.

How do ghosts like their drinks?
Ice ghoul.

Three old and rather deaf friends met one day in the centre of town.

"Windy, isn't it?" said the first.

"No, it's Thursday," replied the second.

"So am I," said the third. "Let's go and have a cup of tea."

What did the dirt say to the rain?
If this keeps up, my name will be mud.

What makes a football pitch wet?
The players' dribbling.

MAISIE: Have you heard the story about the fog?
DAISY: Yes, it's all over town.

Why shouldn't you tell a joke when you go ice-skating?
Because the ice might crack up.

Have you read:
Living at the North Pole by I. C. Blast
and
Living at the South Pole by Anne Tarctic?